MW01054733

THE BIBLE IS BLACK HISTORY

ABC's

THE BIBLE ALPHABET

ISBN: 9798667149767

Front cover image by Tanya Roberts & Nike Adewumi.
Book design by Tanya Roberts.

www.bibleisblackhistory.com

This book is dedicated to my grandchildren
Kira and Kaulin Williams, our future

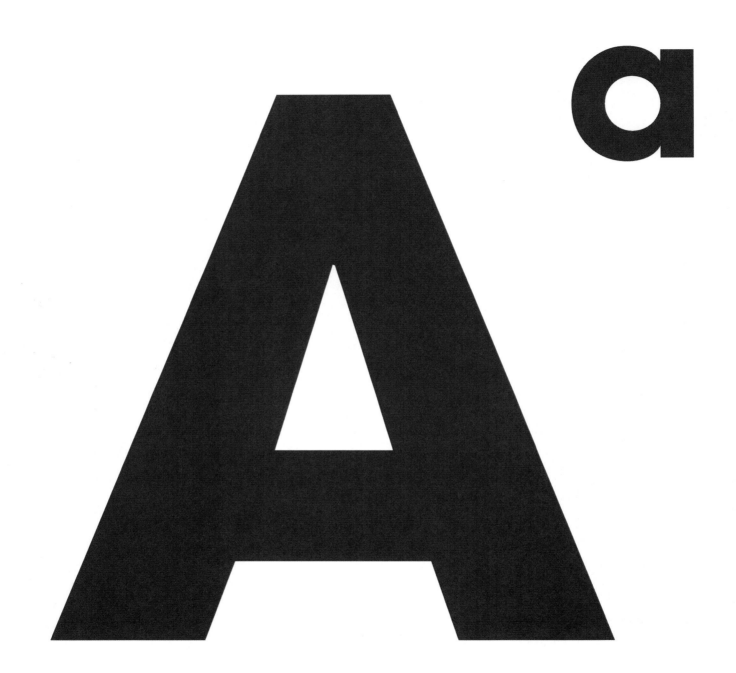

Adam

The First Man of Creation
The Father of Humanity

Bb

Bathsheba

The Mother of Solomon,
The wisest man who ever lived

Christ

The Son of God

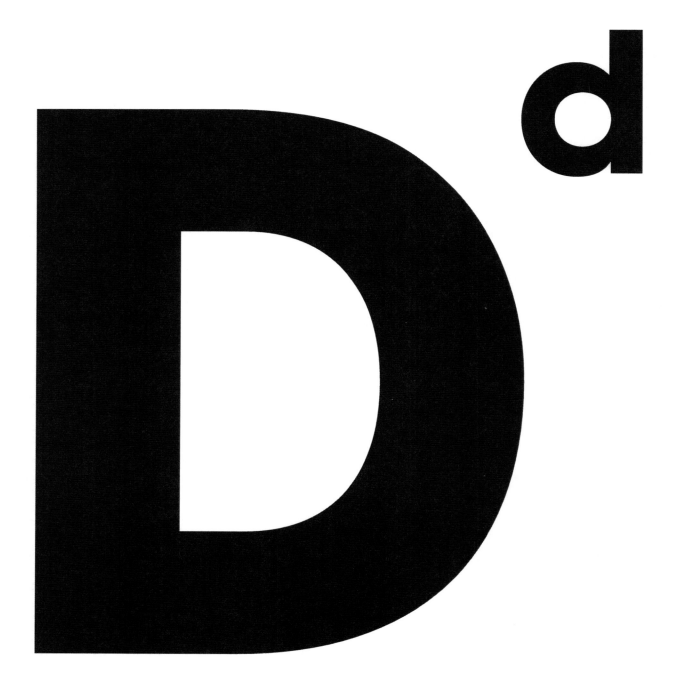

Deborah

The only Woman
Judge of Israel

Eve

The Mother of
All that Lived

Father Abraham

The Father of
the Hebrew People

Gg

Gideon

The Great Judge of Israel

Hosea

The Prophet of Israel

Immanuel

God is with Us

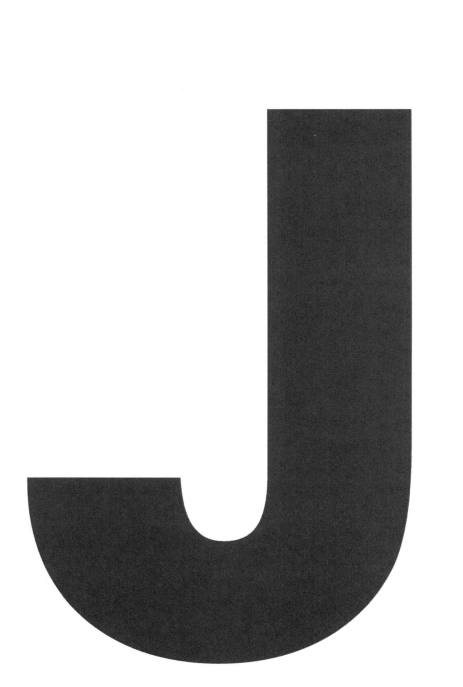

Jesus

Savior of the World

K k

Kish

**The Father of Saul,
Israel's First King**

Lydia

The First Christian
Businesswoman

Mary

The Mother of Jesus

Noah

**Built the Ark that Saved the
Human Race from the Flood**

Obadiah

A Worshipper
and Servant of God

Pp

Paul

The Great Apostle
to the Gentiles

Queen Esther

Saved the Hebrew
People from Destruction

Ruth

The Great Grandmother
of King David

Sarah

The Mother of the
Hebrew People

Timothy

Paul's Spiritual Son and Preacher of the Gospel

U u

Uriah

A Brave Soldier in the Israelite Army

Vashti

The Beautiful Queen of Persia

Wise Men

**Traveled from afar to
Worship the Baby Jesus**

Xerxes

The King of Persia

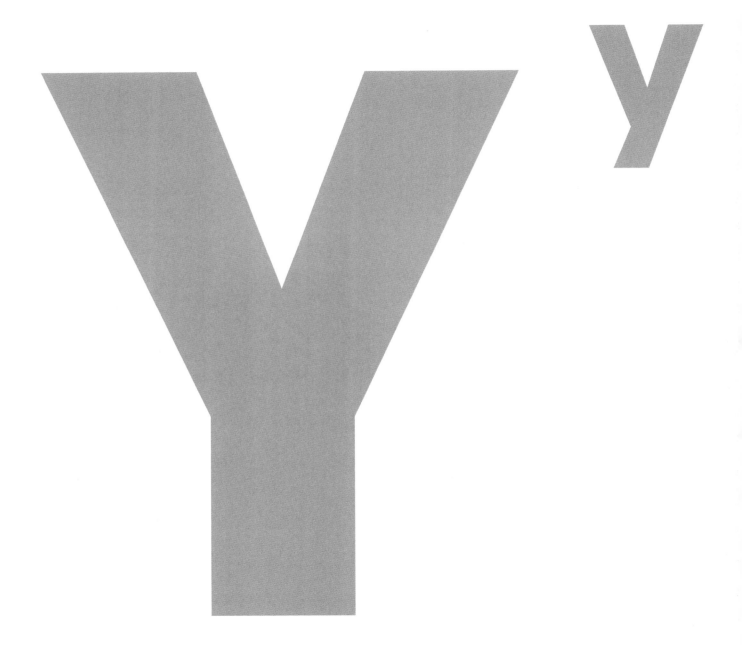

Yahweh

The God of Heaven and Earth

Zachariah

The Father of John
the Baptist

A is for **Adam**, the Garden of Eden was his home;

B is for Bathsheba, the mother of Solomon, the wisest king to sit on the throne.

C is for **Christ**, our Savior who won't fail;

D is for **Deborah** the only woman judge of Israel.

E is for **Eve**, the first mom we ever knew;

F is for **Father Abraham**, the first known Hebrew.

G is for **Gideon**, a judge who made sure justice was won;

H is for **Hosea**, the prophet who told of things to come.

I is for **Immanuel**, God is with us is what it means;

J is for **Jesus** the Lord of Lords and the King of Kings

K is for **Kish**, father of Israel's first king, Saul;

L is for **Lydia** the first Christian Businesswoman to sell clothes to all.

M is for **Mary**, the mother of Jesus, who shed His blood;

N is for **Noah** who built the ark for the flood.

O is for **Obadiah**, he worshipped God and served;

P is for **Paul**, the great apostle, who preached God's Word.

Q is for Queen Esther, who saved the Hebrews from an awful fate;

R is for **Ruth**, the great grandmother of King David, the great.

S is for Sarah, for all the Hebrews she is mother;

T is for **Timothy**, who looked up to apostle Paul as a big brother.

U is for **Uriah**, a great soldier, to protect was his duty;

V is for **Vashti**, the queen of Persia with amazing beauty.

W is for the Wise Men, who found the baby Jesus because they followed the star;

X is for Xerxes whose vast Persian empire stretched afar.

Y is for Yahweh, which means God is the maker, He made me, you, the birds and fish;

Z is for Zachariah, the father of John the Baptist.

Renee Ashley Hunt

Reneehtu@gmail.com

New Jersey based Illustrator Renee Hunt creates character artwork in styles ranging from playful and whimsically simple to more realistic and technical images. She is a graduate from Andrews University in Michigan, where she studied oil painting, graphic design, animation and printmaking under the best industry professionals including internationally known artist Harry Ahn. Since then, Renee has been working in New Jersey for five years. Over her career she has created many published illustrations for a list of well-known clients. Today, Renee is engaged with illustrating for client projects in picture books, advertising, fashion, websites and magazines.

Dr. Theron D. Williams

For more than 30 years, Dr. Theron D. Williams has been the Pastor of the Mt. Carmel Church of Indianapolis, Indiana. Dr. Williams was born in Detroit, Michigan. He is an alumnus of Virginia Union University and the Samuel DeWitt Proctor, School of Theology at Virginia Union, earning a Bachelor of Arts and a Master of Divinity degree, respectively. Dr. Williams is also a graduate of The Chicago Theological Seminary, receiving a Doctor of Ministry Degree. Dr. Williams is the founder and president of The Bible is Black History Institute, LLC. Its mission is to educate communities of African descent of their biblical heritage. Dr. Williams is the author of twelve books, including: The Bible is Black History; The Bible is Black History Personal Workbook; The Bible is Black History Children's Edition; The Bible Alphabet Book for Children; The Bible is Black History Children's Activities Book; The Bible is Black History: Young Heroes of the Bible; The Bible is Black History: Great Women of the Bible.

Made in the USA
Middletown, DE
24 May 2021